Cambridge English

FUN for Starters

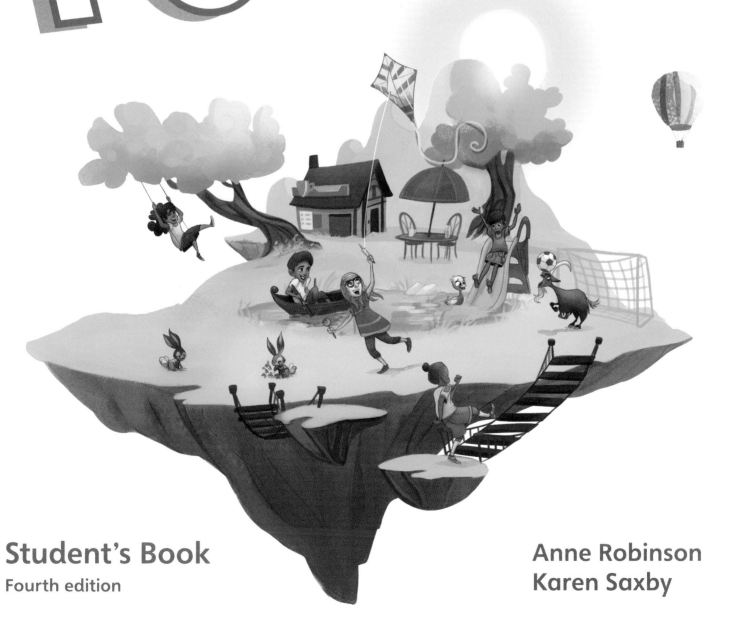

Student's Book
Fourth edition

Anne Robinson
Karen Saxby

Cambridge University Press
www.cambridge.org/elt

Cambridge Assessment English
www.cambridgeenglish.org

Information on this title: www.cambridge.org/9781316631911

© Cambridge University Press 2016

First published 2006
Second edition 2010
Third edition 2015
Fourth edition 2016

40 39 38 37 36 35 34 33

Printed in Malaysia by Vivar Printing

A catalogue record for this publication is available from the British Library

ISBN 978-1-316-61746-5 Student's Book with online activities with audio and Home Fun Booklet
ISBN 978-1-316-63191-1 Student's Book with online activities with audio
ISBN 978-1-316-61749-6 Teacher's Book with downloadable audio
ISBN 978-1-108-72816-4 Presentation Plus

The authors and publishers would like to thank the ELT professionals who commented on the material at different stages of its development.

The authors are grateful to: Niki Donnelly of Cambridge University Press.

Anne Robinson would like to give special thanks to Adam Evans and to many, many teachers and students who have inspired her along the way. Gratitude to her parents Margaret and Jim - her first teachers, who definitely encouraged her to discover and have fun! Warm thanks to José Ramón for his patience and understanding while this series was being written and Cristina and Victoria for their help and enthusiasm. And in memory of her brother Dave.

Karen Saxby would like to give special thanks to everyone she has worked with at Cambridge Assessment since the birth of YLE! She would particularly like to mention Frances, Felicity and Ann Kelly. She would also like to acknowledge the enthusiasm of all the teachers she has met through her work in this field. And lastly, Karen would like to say a big thank you to her sons, Tom and William, for bringing constant FUN and creative thinking to her life and work.

Freelance editorial services by Christine Barton

Design and typeset by Wild Apple Design.

Cover design by Chris Saunders (Astound).

Sound recordings by dsound Recording Studios, London

The authors and publishers acknowledge the following sources of copyright material and are grateful for the permissions granted. While every effort has been made, it has not always been possible to identify the sources of all the material used, or to trace all copyright holders. If any omissions are brought to our notice, we will be happy to include the appropriate acknowledgements on reprinting and in the next update to the digital edition, as applicable.

The authors and publishers are grateful to the following illustrators:

T = Top, B = Below, L = Left, R = Right, C = Centre, B/G = Background

Laetitia Aynié (Sylvie Poggio Artists Agency) pp. 23 (C), 44 (T), 58 (C), 81 (T), 87 (T); David Banks pp. 58, 86 (B), 99 (B); Adrian Bijoo@Advocate 59, 82 (T), 88 (B); Joanna Boccardo pp. 33 (C), 84 (T); Chris Embleton-Hall (Advocate Art) pp. 11 (T), 17 (C), 41 (B), 48, 67 (T), 76 (B), 94 (B); Andrew Elkerton (Sylvie Poggio Artists Agency) pp. 7, 9 (B), 13 (T), 16 (B), 17 (T, B), 33 (T), 34, 35, 54, 71 (T), 72 (T), 74 (C), 75 (B), 82 (C), 89, 94 (T); Clive Goodyer pp. 18, 19 (T), 25 (T), 26 (B), 27, 32 (B), 38 (B), 43 (B), 45, 69, 72 (B), 76 (T), 80 (T), 86 (T); Andrew Hamilton @ Elephant Shoes Ink Ltd pp. 13 (B), 15 (T, B), 20 (T), 26, 32 (T), 41 (T), 44 (C), 46 (B), 47 (T), 61 (C, B), 68 (B), 78 (T), 84 (C), 88 (C); Brett Hudson (Graham-Cameron Illustration) pp. 19 (B), 37 (T), 49 (C), 50 (B), 53 (T), 79 (T); Kelly Kennedy (Sylvie Poggio Artists Agency) pp. 9 (T), 39 (T), 46 (T), 47 (B), 51 (T), 66, 68 (T), 73, 82 (B), 85; Nigel Kitching pp. 18 (T), 25 (C), 43 (T), 49 (B), 53 (BL), 57 (T), 61, 97 (T); Arpad Olbey (Beehive Illustration) pp. 19 (C), 10, 24 (B), 71 (B, C), 84 (B), 87 (B); Nina de Polonia (Advocate Art) pp. 10, 44 (B), 50 (T), 62, 80 (B), 82 (T), 88 (B), 93 (B); David Pratt pp. 37 (B); Anthony Rule monkey and Project bag images throughout, pp. 5, 6, 11, 14, 18, 19, 22, 26, 31, 32, 38, 41, 46, 50, 55, 58, 62, 66, 68, 72, 74, 76, 78, 82, 86, 87, 90, 94; Pip Sampson pp. 15 (C), 29, 30, 38 (T), 40, 43 (C), 56, 57 (B), 63, 70, 71 (B), 74, 78 (B), 79 (B), 90; Melanie Sharp (Sylvie Poggio Artists Agency) pp. 6 (B), 8, 11 (R), 16 (T), 22, 23 (B), 37 (C), 52, 53 (BR), 60, 64, 65, 73, 77, 83, 88, 95, 97 (C, B), 99 (T); Emily Skinner pp. 57 (B); Jo Taylor pp. 20 (B), 21, 28, 31, 39 (B), 42, 58 (B), 74 (B), 75 (T), 81 (B), 84 (B), 91, 92; Theresa Tibbetts pp. 93 (T, C); Matt Ward @ Beehive pp. 51, 63; Sue Wimperis (Graham-Cameron Illustration) pp. 67 (B); Sue Woollatt (Graham-Cameron Illustration) pp. 14, 34, 96, 98.

Contents

1 Say hello!

A Hello! Say, spell and write names.

My name is ....

What's your name? ....

B ▶ Know your letters!

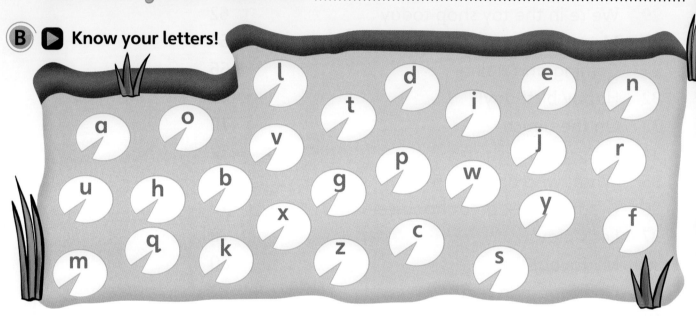

C Draw a red line (a–z) from the baby spider to its dad!

a	b	k	b	t	g	q
l	x	c	s	m	q	r	n
p	y	d	e	f	g	b	v
n	o	c	s	z	h	w	m
a	w	v	k	j	i	u	f
e	y	i	l	g	v	w	x
f	o	n	m	h	u	j	y
x	p	q	r	s	t	k	z

D ▶ Listen! Draw a line from the baby frog to its mum!

E **What's this? Write the word.**

Example .... fish ....
1 ....
2 ....

3 ....
4 ....
5 ....

Letter jumbles:
f h s i (example)
1 d k c u
2 h s e e p
3 o f r g
4 g t a o
5 p i r d s e

F ▶ **What's the animal?**
1 <u>g</u> <u>o</u> a <u>t</u>
2 _ _ e _ _
3 _ _ i _ _ _
4 _ _ o _
5 _ u _ _

Do you know these animals too?
This cat's name is ....
This dog's name is ....
This snake's name is ....

_ a _
_ o _
_ _ a _ e

G *Funtime* **Play the game! Can you make a word?**

2 Numbers, numbers, numbers

A Write the numbers.

two ....2....   five ....   **seven** ....

eight ....   nine ....   ten ....

eleven ....   **twelve** ....   thirteen ....

fifteen ....   twenty ....

B Look at the letters. Write words for six things in the picture.

r C a

1 d b e

2 o S k c

c a r

3 e s h o

4 k o b o

5 t a c

_ _ _

_ _ _ _

_ _ _ _

6

_ _ _ _

_ _ _ _ _ _ _

C Let's count! How many can you see? Answer the questions.

How many cats are there in the picture? ....3....

How many balls are there? ....

How many shoes are there? ....

8

D ▶ **Listen and write a name or a number.**

Examples

What is the boy's name?	.... Tom ....
How old is he?	.... 9 ....
1 How many toys has Tom got?	....
2 What is the name of Tom's cat?	....
3 How many books has Tom got?	....
4 What is the name of Tom's school?	.... School
5 Which class is Tom in?	....

E **Listen and draw lines between the letters and numbers.**

F **Colour and draw.**

Colour **B** brown. Colour **G** green.
And draw a big yellow sun in the picture!

G *Funtime* **Play number games!**

3 What's your name?

A **Look at the letters. Write the names.**

1 ~~HeB~~
  B e n

2 s ᵐ a
  _ _ _

3 ᶜ L ᵘ y
  _ _ _ _

4 k ⁱ N ᶜ
  _ _ _ _

5 B ₗ ⁱ ˡ
  _ _ _ _

6 a ⁿ A ₙ
  _ _ _ _

7 ʳ a M k
  _ _ _ _

8 i ᵐ K
  _ _ _

9

B **Write the names under *boy*, *girl* or *boy and girl*.**

~~Dan~~ Alex Sue Matt
Alice Jill May Pat Grace

........Dan........ ....
....
....
....
....
....
....

My favourite English names are:

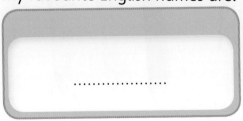

....

and

....

C ▶ **Listen and write the names.**

1 ....Tom........   3 Mr ....   5 ....

2 ....   4 ....   6 Mrs ....

D Answer the questions. Write your names in the circle.

1 What's your name?
2 What's your friend's name?
3 What's your grandmother's name?
4 What's a good name for a cat or a dog?

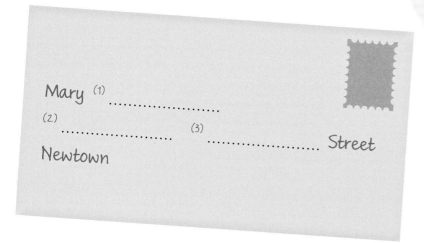

E ▶ Listen and write the names and numbers.

Mary (1) ....
(2)
.... (3)
.... Street
Newtown

F It's your friend's birthday!
Write your friend's name and address.

....
....
....

G Find a name from A, B or C in these sentences.

1 Listen to my story!
2 The cat is sleeping on the mat today.
3 She wants an orange and an apple.
4 Grandma, you're great!
5 Be nice to your teacher!
6 Stop at the end of the street.

H Funtime Play the game! Names bingo.

PROJECT

4 Red, blue and yellow

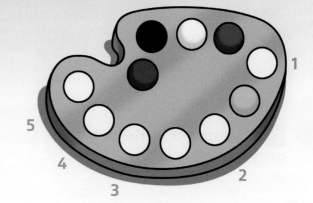

A Read and colour.

1. blue + red = ...
2. white + black = ...
3. blue + yellow = ...
4. yellow + red = ...
5. red + white = ...

B You and colours. Answer the questions.

What colour are your eyes?

What colour is your T-shirt?

What colour is your bedroom?

What colour is your hair?

What is your favourite colour?

Me	My Friend	
☐	☐	
☐	☐	
☐	☐	
☐	☐	
☐	☐	

C Look at the pictures. Circle the correct word.

1. This is a boat / goat.
2. This is a cat / mat.
3. This is a kite / tree.
4. This is a boy / woman.

D ▶ **Listen and colour the birds.**

E Great colours for a car, shoes, sports shoes, ice cream or bike!

What's a good colour for a  ?   What colour do you like?

What colour are your favourite  ?   What's a great colour for a ?

What colour is your favourite ?

5 Answering questions

A Complete the crossword. Find the answers in the box.

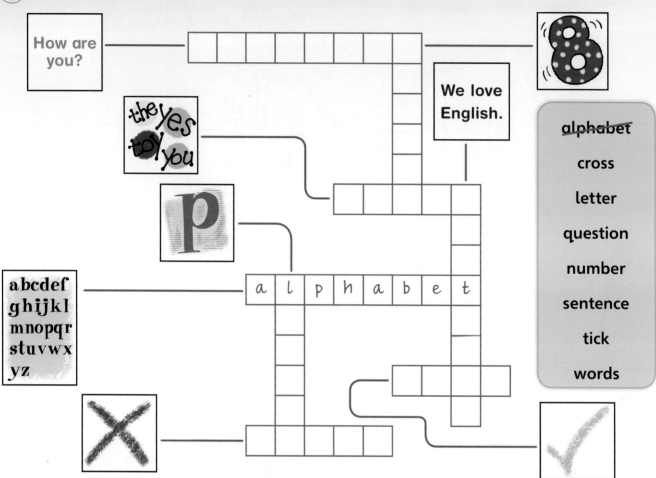

alphabet
cross
letter
question
number
sentence
tick
words

B Read, draw and write.

1 Draw a line.

2 Tick the box.

3 Write yes.

4 Write a number.

5 Put a cross in the box.

6 Write one word.

7 What's your favourite English word? ....

8 Write a sentence with five words. ....

9 Write a question with four words. ....

14

Pat   Ben   Kim   Hugo

Eva   Mark   Sam

Examples

One of the boys is sleeping.   ....yes..........

The girl in the tree has black hair.   ....no..........

Questions

1   You can see six apples.   ....

2   The dog is brown and white.   ....

3   The children are in the house.   ....

4   The boy's ball is purple.   ....

5   The frog is on a book.   ....

D ▶ **Listen and draw lines.**

E *Funtime* **Mime the sentence.**

6 Animals and aliens

A Write the animals, then draw lines from *a* or *an*.

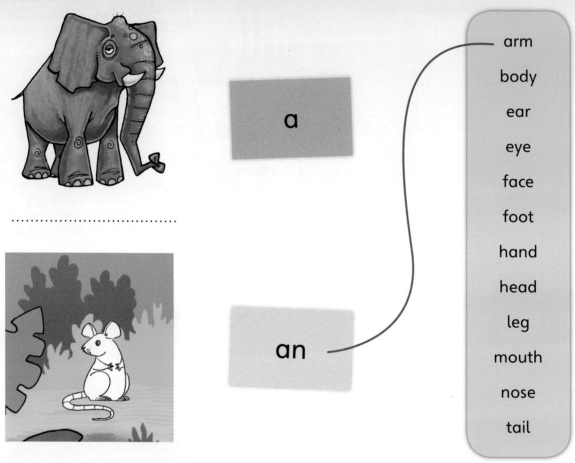

a

an

arm

body

ear

eye

face

foot

hand

head

leg

mouth

nose

tail

....

....

B Look and read. Put a tick (✔) or a cross (✗) in the box.

1   This is a hand. ☒

2   This is a nose. ☐

3   This is an eye. ☐

4   This is a leg. ☐

5   This is a mouth. ☐

6   These are arms. ☐

7   This is a head. ☐

8   This is a tail. ☐

9   These are feet. ☐

10   This is an _ _ _ _ _ _ !

C Read this. Choose a word from the box. Write the correct word next to numbers 1–5.

You can see giraffes at the .... zoo .... Giraffes are very big (1) .... Giraffes have got four long (2) .... and their tails are very long too. Giraffes see with their big brown (3) .... They like eating (4) .... , but they don't eat meat. They drink (5) .... Their bodies are yellow, orange and brown. Giraffes are fantastic animals. Do you like giraffes?

Example

zoo   water   legs   animals

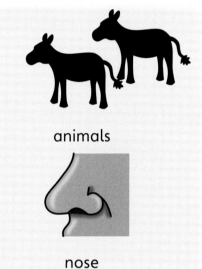

fruit   shoe   eyes   nose

D Write one word on the lines.

This is a .... and it's a very .... animal.
It runs with its .... legs and it has
a very long ....
It likes eating .... but it doesn't eat meat.
It drinks .... and it loves swimming in it too!
Horses are really cool! Can you ride one?

E *Funtime* Play two games!

Make the animals!

Have you got the lizard's tail?

7 Look, listen, smile, draw

A Look at the pictures. Look at the letters. Write the words.

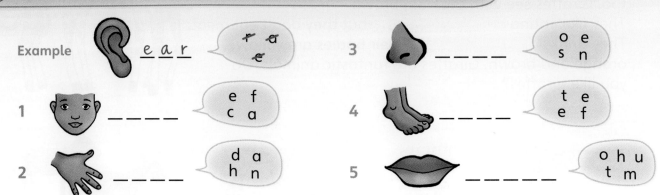

Example e a r `r a e`   3 _ _ _ _ `o e s n`

1 _ _ _ _ `e f c a`   4 _ _ _ _ `t e e f`

2 _ _ _ _ `d a h n`   5 _ _ _ _ _ `o h u t m`

B What's not there? Write the parts of the face.

1 his ...ears...   2 her ....   3 his ....   4 his ....   5 her ....

C Choose and write the correct word.

1 I .... with my mouth.
2 I .... and .... with my eyes.
3 I .... to music with my ears.
4 I .... at my friends with my hand.
5 I can .... a ball with my feet and I can ....
with my feet and legs.

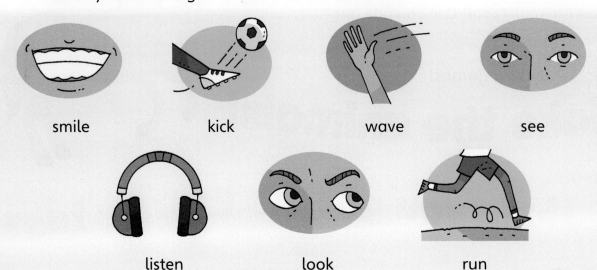

smile   kick   wave   see

listen   look   run

D Look at Sam's robot. Choose and write words on the lines.

> ~~computer~~ clock   keyboard   kites   socks

1 The ....computer.... is the robot's face.
2 The .... is the robot's mouth.
3 The .... is the robot's body.
4 The .... are the robot's arms.
5 The .... are the robot's legs.

Now draw the robot's eyes, ears and nose.

E Look at the picture. Find words to complete the sentences.

> ~~smiling~~ frog   tail   hand   boxes   ball   waving

The family are ....smiling........ . But they aren't sitting on chairs! The boy's (1) .... from the tree! Can you see the (2) .... under his sister? The old man and woman are sitting on two (3) .... The baby's got a flower in her (4) .... and she and her mum are sitting on a big (5) .... The cat's on the shoe! Can you see its brown (6) .... ?

F *Funtime* **Play the game! Draw the monkey.**

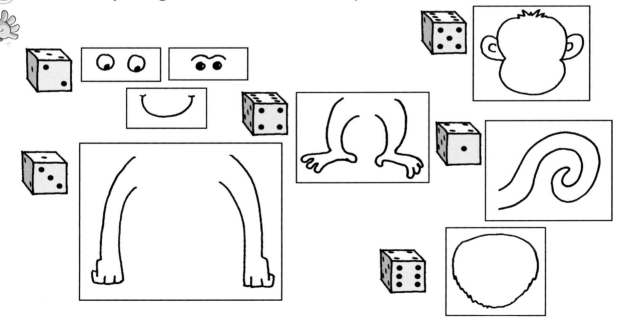

8 In my clothes cupboard

A Write the words for the pictures.

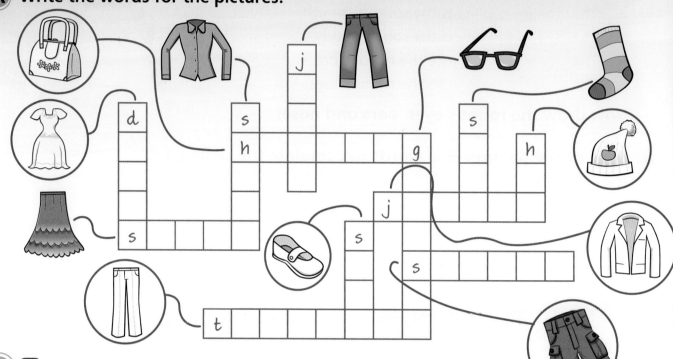

B ▶ Listen and tick (✔) the box.

1   Which boy is Tom?

A ☐   B ☐   C ☐

2   Which is Kim's dad?

A ☐   B ☐   C ☐

3   Which woman is Dan's teacher?

A ☐   B ☐   C ☐

4   Where is the T-shirt?

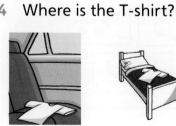

A ☐   B ☐   C ☐

C Look at the picture. Write one-word answers to the questions.

Examples

What colour is the boy's T-shirt? _red_

How many sofas are there? _one_

1 Where is the jacket? on the ....

2 How many people are there in the picture? ....

3 What colour is the woman's skirt? ....

4 What is the baby wearing on one of her feet? a blue ....

5 What colour is the girl's hair? ....

D Count and then make sentences. Use There is or There are.

1 | four | There are | green | chairs |

....

2 | white | There are | two | lamps |

....

3 | baby | There is | one | happy |

....

4 | .... | .... | cats | .... |

....

5 | .... | .... | .... | flowers |

....

E Funtime Play the game! The long clothes sentence.

21

9 Funny monsters

A Look, read and write numbers. Then, draw and colour the clothes.

The monster

It's got ....2........... heads and .... eyes. It's got .... noses. It hasn't got a mouth, but it's got .... funny tails.

Its .... feet are very big. Its .... arms are very long and its hands are very small.

Today it's wearing baseball caps and boots and a big T-shirt.

B Read and colour the monster.

1 The monster's arms are red and its hands are green.
2 It's got purple faces, pink eyes and yellow noses.
3 Colour three boots blue and two boots orange.
4 Make its T-shirt pink and its baseball caps orange.

C Choose words and write about the monster!

Say 'Hello' to Bounce!
It's very big/small, happy/sad, very beautiful/ugly, scary/silly and really funny!
It drinks .... and .... is its favourite food!

D **Which monster am I? Look at our pictures. Write the correct number.**

1	I've got a flower in my hair.	monster ....4.........
2	I'm holding my baby.	monster ....
3	I love reading funny stories.	monster ....
4	I've got my robot in my hand.	monster ....
5	I really like my new glasses!	monster ....

The monster picture hall

....

E **Look at the monsters. Write colours.**

Monster	body	hair	eyes	nose	arms	feet
1	blue	black	red	blue	0	red
2						
3						
4						

F **Write names for monsters 1–4 under the pictures in the Picture Hall.**

G **Listen and complete the sentences about monster 5.**

Hi! My name's .... I love reading
.... stories and learning about ....
in the .... at my new school.

H ▶ *Funtime* **Play the game! Colour the wall.**

What's that?

It's a funny monster!

10 Our families

A **Read about Sam. Which picture is Sam's family?**

My name's Sam. I live in a big house with my (mum) and dad and my three sisters and two brothers. My grandpa and grandma live in the small blue house next to us. We all love animals. We've got a donkey. Its name is Mango. Our dog's name is Chocolate and he plays and sleeps in our garden. My grandparents have got a cat and three fish. The cat's name is Lucy but I don't know the names of their fish!

1    2    3

B **Put circles round the family words.**

C **Complete the sentences about Sam's family's pets.**

This is our
....

These are our
....

This is my
....

....
my favourite
....

24

D Answer the questions.

1   Is your street long or short? ....
2   How many people live in your house/flat? ....
3   Do your grandfathers and grandmothers live with you? ....
4   Have you got a lot of cousins? ....
5   Has your family got a pet? ....

E Draw circles round words about your family and home and write names.

This is me!

My name's ....

I live in a | big small | house flat |

with my | mum dad brother sister grandma grandpa grandparents | .

.... | lives live | in the | house flat |

next to us.

We love | animals cats dogs gardens | , but we haven't got a

| cat   dog   garden | !

F 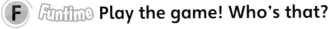 Play the game! Who's that?

25

11 Whose is it?

Look and read. Put a tick (✔) or a cross (✗) in the box.

Examples

These are eyes. ✔

This is a skateboard. ✗

Questions

1  This is a robot. ☐

4  This is a cake. ☐

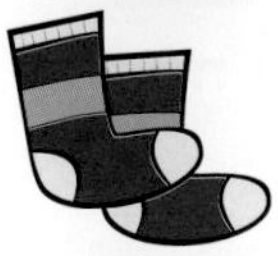

2 These are socks. ☐

5  This is a keyboard. ☐

3 This is a name. ☐

6  This is a tablet. ☐

B Look, read and write answers.

1	Whose mouse is it?	It's Nick's.	It's his.
2	Whose watch is it?	It's	It's hers.
3	Whose tennis ball is it?	It's	It's
4	Whose clock is it?	It's	It's
5	Whose kite is it?	It's	It's
6	Whose paints are they?	They're	They're

C ▶ Listen. What have the five friends got? Draw lines.

D Are they his or hers?

Bill has got five things in this cupboard. His favourite colour is red. Bill likes taking photos and drawing.

Jill has got four things. She likes music, doing sport and going to the beach.

The ...., ..., ...,
.... and the .... are Bill's things.
The ...., ..., ... and the
.... are Jill's things.

E *Funtime* Play the games! What have you got?

12 Who's got the red balloon?

A Find the words and write them on the lines under the picture.

womenrlgirliababyprowomantkidsaboyrotmangbochildrenmen

b _ _ _ b _ _ g _ _ _ c _ _ _ _ _ _ _ _

m _ _ m _ _ w _ _ _ _ w _ _ _ _ k _ _ _

B Write yes or no.

Examples

Two girls have got a duck. ...yes...   The men have got a ball. ...no...

Questions

1 A boy has got a kite. ....   7 Two men have got a duck. ....

2 A man has got a horse. ....   8 A boy has got a book. ....

3 A woman has got a book. ....   9 A woman has got a
                                            handbag. ....

4 A girl has got an ice cream. ....

5 A baby has got a horse. ....   10 Two women have got

6 A man has got a dog. ....   some flowers. ....

C Ask and answer questions about people.

Is your best friend a boy or a girl?

a ....

Is your English teacher a man or a woman?

a ....

How many people are there in your family?

....

How many children are there in your class?

....

D Look at the pictures and answer the questions.

Examples

How many kids are there?
.............2.............
What is the boy watching?
the ....television....
1 What is the girl doing?
....

2 What does the boy want?   his ....
3 Where is the girl looking?   behind the ....
4 Where are the kids now?   in the ....
5 Who has got the phone?   the ....

E *Funtime* Play the game! Nine lives.

13 Who can do this?

A Five funny monsters!
Look at the ticks (✔)
and crosses (✗).

	fly	swim	read	jump	run	sing
Alphabet	✔	✗	✗	✔	✔	✗
Bean	✗	✗	✗	✗	✗	✔
Carrot	✗	✗	✔	✔	✔	✔
Doll						
Egg	✗	✔	✗	✗	✗	✗

Alphabet

Bean

Carrot

Doll

Egg

Which monster? Write the names.

1 He can sing but he can't run, read, fly, swim or jump. ....

2 She can jump, run, sing and read but she can't fly or swim ....

3 He can't fly or read or jump or run or sing but he can swim! ....

B ▶ **Listen and tick (✔) the box.**

What is Egg doing now?

A ☐

B ☐

C ☐

1 Where is Doll?

A ☐

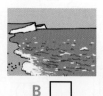
B ☐

C ☐

2 Where is Bean singing?

A ☐

B ☐

C ☐

3 What is Carrot reading about?

A ☐

B ☐

C ☐

4 What can Egg's baby brother do?

A ☐

B ☐

C ☐

5 What can Alphabet draw?

A ☐

B ☐

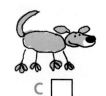
C ☐

C Read about me and my classmates. Write our names.

Kim has got a really big garden. He can play badminton with his dad there.

Lucy can ride a horse. She's really good at riding horses.

I love Anna's paintings. They're so cool! She draws fantastic pictures!

Nick likes riding his bike. He can ride his bike to school.

Dan has got a new camera. He can take really good photos.

My name's May. I can play the guitar very well. Can you see my guitar?

Bill's good at singing. He writes funny songs and sings them in class!

Grace loves fishing. She's got a boat and catches lots of fish in the sea.

Alice has got a new tennis racket. She plays tennis with her sister.

Mr Page is our teacher. He's really good at swimming. We can have a swimming lesson now!

1 ......Alice......	2	3 ....
4	5	6 ....
7	8	9 ....
10		

D Funtime Play the game! Stand up. Sit down again.

14 Big, small, happy or sad?

A Look and answer the questions.

1 What's this?   a _ _ _ _ _ _ _ _
2 Have you got a ....?
3 Is this .... big or small?

1 What are these?   _ _ _ _ _ _
2 Are you wearing .... today?
3 Are these .... long or short?

1 What's this?   a _ _ _ _ _ _
2 What colour is this ....?
3 Is this .... old or new?

1 What are these?   _ _ _ _ _ _ _ _ _ _
2 Do you wear .... to school?
3 Are these .... clean or dirty?

Balloons: r c u t m p o e / o s c k s / e n p h o / r s e o t s s u r

B Write the word under the picture.

beautiful young ugly old short ~~clean~~ long dirty old new

1 a ...clean... car
2 a .... car
3 an .... shoe
4 a .... shoe
5 a .... woman
6 an .... woman
7 a .... spider
8 an .... spider
9 a .... skirt
10 a .... skirt

C Choose words and draw pictures.

A	big	boy	is drawing a	red	snake.
	sad	girl	is painting a	blue	computer.
	funny	zebra	is holding a	yellow	kite.
	small	cat	is playing with a	black	fish.
	happy	elephant	is riding a	green	alien.
	short	mouse	is watching a	white	balloon.

D Look and read. Write yes or no.

Anna **Eva** **Hugo** **Pat**

Examples

The small dog is happy. ...yes....

The big ball is in the dog's mouth. ....no....

1 The girl in the blue dress is sad. ....

2 One boy is wearing red shoes. ....

3 One of the girls is eating an ice cream. ....

4 The boy with dirty hands is smiling. ....

5 These children are in a house. ....

E Read, write and draw lines.

1 Pat's wearing ......jeans........ and a blue and white T-shirt.

2 Anna's got long brown .... She's wearing a blue dress. She's happy today.

3 Eva's got a chocolate ice cream. She's wearing ....

4 Hugo's playing with Pat. Hugo's wearing ....

F Funtime Play the game! Opposites bingo.

15 One, two, three animals

A Match animal numbers and animal words.

1

(5) chicken .... small, brown, walk ....

( ) donkey ....

2

( ) snake ....

( ) frog ....

3

( ) hippo ....

( ) polar bear ....

4

( ) spider ....

( ) sheep ....

5

( ) jellyfish ....

( ) cow ....

6

( ) crocodile ....

( ) tiger ....

7

( ) zebra ....

( ) lizard ....

8

( ) goat ....

9

10

11

12

13

14

15

B Write words next to the animals.

big	black	grey	red
long	blue	orange	white
beautiful	brown	pink	yellow
short	green	purple	
ugly			
small			

fly
jump
run
swim
walk

C   **Where are Tom's pets? Draw lines.**

1	in the box
2	on the ball
3	in the shoe
4	under the kite
5	on the cap
6	in the water

D   **Talk about the picture.**

Where's?   What's?   How many?   What colour?   What's he / she / it doing?

E   *Funtime* **Play the game! At the zoo.**

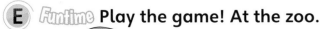

A Look at the pictures. Write the words.

apple ~~apple~~
banana
beans
carrot
coconut
grapes
lemon
lime
mango
onion
orange
pea
pear
pineapple
potato
tomato
watermelon
kiwi

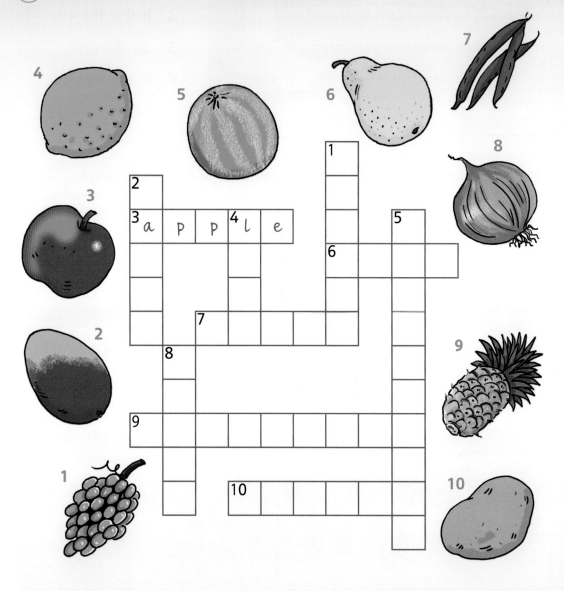

Crossword: 3 across: a p p l e

B What is it?

1 It's a fruit. It's long and yellow. Monkeys like it.   It's a ......banana......
2 It's very small and green, but it's not a bean.   It's a ....
3 It's brown and white. There's lots of milk in it.   It's a ....
4 It's yellow. You can make a great drink from it.   It's a ....
5 It's a fruit and a colour. You can make fruit juice from it.   It's an ....
6 It's red and round. Some people put it on pizzas.   It's a ....
7 It's long and orange and horses love eating it.   It's a ....
8 It's green and black but it's not a grape.   It's a ....

C Spell and say *tomatoes* and *potatoes!*

t o m a _ _ _ _ _

p o t a _ _ _ _ _

D ▶ What's in Ben's funny fruit drink?

Tick (✔) five boxes.

pear ☐
tomato ☐
carrot ☐
orange ☐
apple ☐
grapes ☐
mango ☐
banana ☐
lemon ☐

What's in your drink?

.... , ... , ... , ... and .... !

E Talk about the picture.

1 Where's the coconut?
2 Where are the lizards?
3 What's this?

4 What colour is the .... ?
5 How many .... are there?
6 What's the bird standing on?

F *Funtime* Play the game! Say it three times.

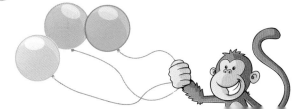

17 What's on the menu?

A Write the menu. Add your favourite lunch, too!

Today's menu

For lunch, try our
- burger and chips
- ....
- ....
- ....
- ....
- ....

onions
potatoes
sausages
chicken
fish
rice
tomatoes
eggs
meatballs

B Write the drinks.

w t a r e
water

c i j u e
_ _ _ _ _

m k i l
_ _ _ _

d m e o l n a e
_ _ _ _ _ _ _ _

h l o a c c t e o
hot _ _ _ _ _ _ _ _

C ▶ **Listen and tick (✔) Lucy's lunch and Matt's lunch.**

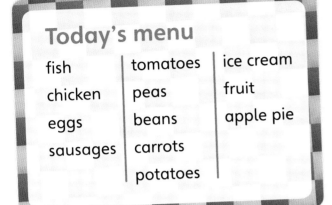

Today's menu

fish	tomatoes	ice cream
chicken	peas	fruit
eggs	beans	apple pie
sausages	carrots	
	potatoes	

D **Write Matt's lunch.**

So, what would you like for lunch, Matt?

.... and ....
today. And can I have
some .... too?

E **What would you like for lunch? Write your words.**

Now, what would you like for lunch?

.... and ....
today. And can I have
some .... too?

F ▶ **Listen and draw lines.**

Sam   Alice   Hugo   Eva

Sue   Bill   Grace

G **Talk about the picture.**

18 A colourful house

A **Look at the house. What colour are these rooms?**

bedroom   bathroom   hall   dining room   living room   kitchen

B ▶ **Listen and draw lines.**

1 .... clock ....

2 ....

3 ....

4 ....

5 ....

6 ....

7 ....

C **Look, read and write one-word answers about the house.**

1 Where's the photo?   It's in the .... hall ....
2 Where's the mat?   It's in the ....
3 Where's the clock?   It's in the ....
4 Where's the lamp?   It's in the ....
5 Where's the mirror?   It's in the ....

D Read and write! Which home words can you see in the mirrors?

Example ....wall........ 1 .... 2 ....

3 .... 4 .... 5 ....

E Read this. Choose a word from the box. Write the correct word next to numbers 1–5.

A desk

A desk has four ....legs........ but it isn't an animal like a
(1)..................... or a zebra.

Some children have a desk in their (2)..................... . They sit
on a (3)..................... and read their favourite (4).....................
there. Some children like putting their crayons, pens and
pencils on their desk.

Some children have a (5)..................... on their desk too, and
play games on it in the evenings.

Example			
legs	computer	chair	stories
bedroom	ear	horse	water

F Write about your home.

My house is in (1)..................... . It's got (2)..................... rooms.
They are: (3)..................... .
My favourite room is (4)..................... .
In my favourite room, you can find (5).....................

....

G Funtime Play the game! The long home sentence.

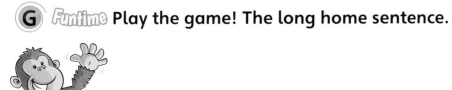

19 What's in your bedroom?

A What can you see in the room? Write the words next to the numbers.

1 a <u>r</u> <u>m</u> <u>c</u> <u>h</u> <u>a</u> <u>i</u> <u>r</u>
2 b _ _ _ _ _ _ _ _
3 c _ _ _ _ _
4 c _ _ _ _ _ _ _ _ _
5 d _ _ _
6 d _ _ _ _
7 p _ _ _ _ _
8 p _ _ _ _ _
9 p _ _ _ _ _ _ _
10 t _ _ _ _ _ _ _ _ _ _ _
11 r _ _
12 w _ _ _ _ _ _

B ▶ Listen and colour.

C What's in your bedroom?

In my bedroom, there's a ...., a ....,
a .... and a ....
....

D Make, write and say two home words!

cup   board

c _ _ _ _ _ _ _ _ _

and an

a _ _ _ _ _ _ _ _

cupboard

a

arm   chair

armchair

E Nick loves fish. Write Nick on the line under his bedroom. Then, complete the sentences about his bedroom.

...................'s room

...................'s room

In Nick's bedroom:

1   the rug is ....orange.......... .
2   the .... is yellow.
3   the .... is red.
4   the walls are ....
5   the .... is blue.
6   the bookcase is ....
7   the .... is big but in Anna's room it's small.

F ▶ Listen and answer questions about Nick.

1   ....
2   ....
3   ....

4   ....
5   ....
6   ....

G *Funtime* Play the game! Guess what I'm drawing.

20 Ben and Kim live here!

A Look and read. Put a tick (✔) or a cross (✗) in the box.

Examples

These are beds. ✔

This is a mouse. ✗

1 This is a kitchen. ☐

2 This is a camera. ☐

3 This is a family. ☐

4 These are shorts. ☐

5 These are cats. ☐

B Write the correct word next to numbers 1–5.

A living room

A living room is part of a ......*house*...... or flat. Lots of
(1) .... sit in a living room in the evenings and watch
(2) .... or listen to music. They sit in (3) ....
or on a sofa. Some people put things like (4) .... or
paintings on the walls of their living room.

Which room is next to your living room? Is it your
(5) .... or the bathroom?

families television posters bed armchairs house kitchen

C Write names and numbers. You choose!

1 The family live in .... Street.
2 The number of their house is ....
3 The boy's name is .... and the girl's name
   is ....
4 .... animals live with this family.

44

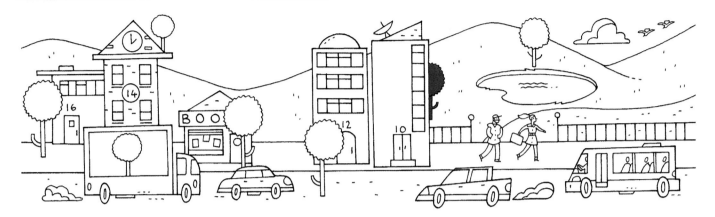

E Read the sentences. Write Ben or Kim.

1   In ....'s street, many houses are small.

2   There are no cars or lorries in ....'s street.

3   There's a bookshop in ....'s street.

4   In ....'s street, the flats are very tall.

5   There's a park behind ....'s street.

6   There are no trees in ....'s street.

7   You can see lots of people in ....'s street.

F Your teacher will give you a photocopy. Write five questions!

Is your garden big or small?

....

....

....

....

21 Play with us!

A Who's playing with the toys? Listen and write names.

Anna
Bill
Dan
Kim
May
Pat
Grace
Jill
Sam
Mark

B You can't ride on or in one of these things. Cross it out!

1	boat	train	~~bean~~	4	hat	helicopter	car
2	bus	box	motorbike	5	lorry	hobby	truck
3	plane	bike	phone	6	skateboard	ship	bear

C What is it?

It goes on the

c	a	r

It goes in the

It goes on the

And it goes on the

▶ **Listen and tick (✔) the box.**

What is Sam riding?

1 What is Anna drawing?

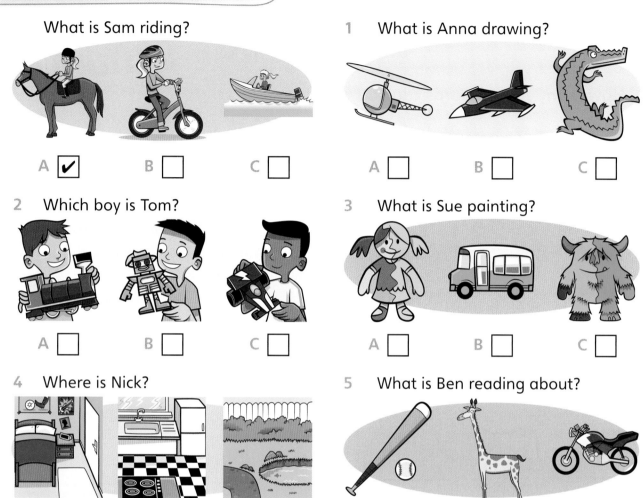

A ✔   B ☐   C ☐

A ☐   B ☐   C ☐

2 Which boy is Tom?

3 What is Sue painting?

A ☐   B ☐   C ☐

A ☐   B ☐   C ☐

4 Where is Nick?

5 What is Ben reading about?

A ☐   B ☐   C ☐

A ☐   B ☐   C ☐

E **Talk about your ride on your flying bike!**

Would you like to ride a flying bike?
    Sit on it now and fly!
        Is it fun? Scary? Fantastic?
    What can you see?
Where are you going?

F **Funtime** **Play the game! Let's make a helicopter crossword.**

22 In our bags and in our school

A How many school words can you find?

b o o k c a s e c u p b o a r d d e s k c r a y o n
p o s t e r t e a c h e r r u l e r e r a s e r
p a p e r b a g c o m p u t e r p e n c i l
k e y b o a r d p a g e m o u s e
r u b b e r t a b l e t

B Write the words for the pictures. Which word can you see in the blue box?

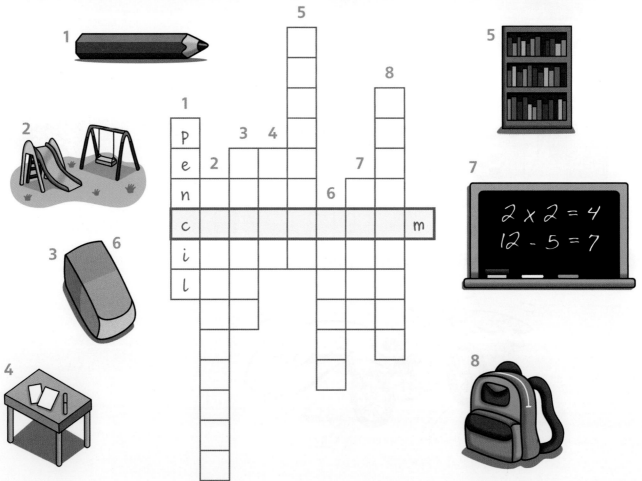

C Write names. Ask your friends and write their answers.

Name:

....

....

....

....

1 So, what colour is your eraser? ....

2 Has your mum or dad got a tablet? ....

3 What's on your desk? ....

4 How many crayons have you got? ....

Pat's bag

Pat's putting his new .... book .... in his school bag. He's putting his
(1) .... and pencils in his bag too. He's taking his new tablet to school
today. That's in his bag, and his (2)..................... is too. He draws lines with
that. Now he's putting an (3)..................... for his lunch in his bag, and some
fruit (4)...................... That's his favourite drink but he likes milk too. Pat wears
(5)..................... at school. Yes. Those are in his bag too.

What's in your school bag today?

Example

book

glasses

juice

shirt

apple

ruler

pens

shells

E Answer questions about Alex's bag.

1   What fruit does Alex have in his bag?
    an apple and a ....
2   How many pencils can you see?
    ....
3   What colour is the ruler?
    ....
4   What can you see behind the apple?
    a ....
5   Where is the bag?
    on the ....
6   What drink can you see?
    some ....

F Funtime Play the game! Close your eyes and draw!

23 At our school

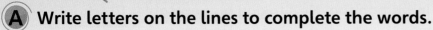

A Write letters on the lines to complete the words.

_ _ _ _ case

_ _ _ _ _ _ _ case

_ _ _ _ _ _ _ case

_ _ _ board

_ _ _ board

_ _ _ _ _ board

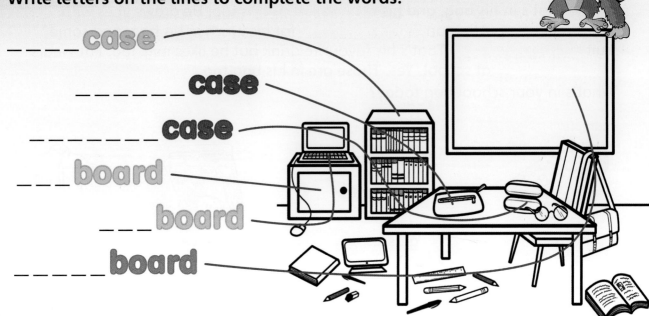

B Whose is it? Write his, her or their.

1

It's .... bag.

2

It's .... ruler.

3

It's .... dog.

C Read the question. Listen and write a name or a number.

Examples

How old is May? .... 8 ....

What is May's brother's name? .... Nick ....

1   Where is May's school? .... Street

2   How many children are there in May's class? ....

3   What is the name of May's friend? ....

4   Who is May's English teacher? Mrs ....

5   What is the number of May's class? ....

D Read about Grace's school and complete the questions.

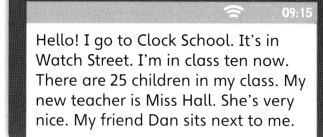

Hello! I go to Clock School. It's in Watch Street. I'm in class ten now. There are 25 children in my class. My new teacher is Miss Hall. She's very nice. My friend Dan sits next to me.

09:15

1 What's the name of your .... ?
2 Where's your .... ?
3 Which .... are you in?
4 How many .... are there in your class?
5 What's your ....'s name?
6 Who do you .... next to?

E Answer the questions from D about *your* school.

Our school

I go to .... school.

My school is in ....

I am in class ....

I have .... classmates.

Our English teacher's name is

....

I sit next to ....

F Read and write yes or no next to the words.

1 It's in a house or classroom.
   a beach ..no..   a flower ....
   a bookcase ....   a computer ....
   a rubber ....   a pencil ....
   a chicken ....   a classmate ....

2 It's on a table.
   a flower ....   a bookcase ....
   a computer ....   a rubber ....
   a pencil ....   a door ....

3 People write, draw and play with it.
   a flower ....   a computer ....
   a rubber ....   a pencil ....

4 It has lots of letters and numbers on its keyboard.
   a computer ....   a pencil ....

   It's a _ _ _ _ _ _ _ _ _ !

24 What's the class doing?

A Listen and answer.

1

2

B Are you looking at picture 1 or picture 2?

1	The teacher is reading a story.	............1...........
2	A boy is eating a banana.	....
3	One girl is jumping.	....
4	The children are sitting down.	....
5	One girl is painting.	....
6	The children are listening to the teacher.	....
7	A boy is sleeping on his desk.	....
8	Two boys are drawing on the board.	....

C Listen to the questions and write one-word answers about picture 2.

What are Tom and Nick doing?
......drawing......

What are they drawing?
a ......rocket......

1 a ....

2 on his ....

3 a ....

4 a ....

D Put the words in the cupboard.

+'ing'
reading

double

goodbye 'e'

I'm eating

We're sitting

They're writ..ing
" e "

read   run   smile   stop   draw   swim   wave   ride   sleep   clap   count

E What are you doing?
I'm doing a crossword.

F What are the children doing now?

Bye!

Hooray!

Anna   Ben   Alex   Nick   Tom   Lucy   Sam

G Funtimo Play the game! Action mimes.

(25) Animal challenge

A Which animals can you see in the picture?
Can you find ten animals?

B ▶ Listen and colour the snakes.

C What can you see in the animal picture?

D ▶ Listen and write.

Tom's pets!

Our guesses

Tom has got three ....

They live in his ....

Tom likes .... with them.   ....

Their names are Lucy, Ben and ....

They eat Tom's mum's ....!   ....

E **Read the sentences and write animal word answers.**

Example

I'm green or brown. You can find me in
and next to water.   a c _ _ _ _ _ _ _ _

1   I'm grey and my body is very fat. I can swim
    but I can walk too.   a h _ _ _ _ _

2   I live in trees. I eat bananas. I've got a tail.   a m _ _ _ _ _ _

3   I'm long. I eat meat. I haven't got legs.   a s _ _ _ _ _

4   I'm small and long. I eat insects. I can run.   a l _ _ _ _ _ _

5   I'm big and white. I can walk on two legs and I
    like eating fish.   a p _ _ _ _ b _ _ _ _

6   I'm grey or brown and I've got really long ears.   a d _ _ _ _ _ _

7   I catch insects and eat them. I've got eight legs.   a s _ _ _ _ _ _

8   I've got four legs and my body is white (or black!). I say Baa!   a s _ _ _ _ _

9   I live in the sea but I don't swim like a fish and I
    don't have a tail.   a j _ _ _ _ _ _ _ _

10 I like meat. I'm orange and black and I've got a tail.   a t _ _ _ _ _

11 I've got four legs and I eat grass. You can get milk from me.   a c _ _ _

12 I eat spiders and flies. I live next to the water. I can jump!   a f _ _ _ _

13 I can run like a horse but my body is black and white.   a z _ _ _ _ _

14 I am small and I fly to flowers. My body is orange and black.   a b _ _ _

F **Project! Where do animals live?**

 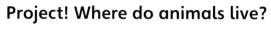

55

26 How many pets?

Examples

What is the girl's name?   May ......_Read_...... .   How old is she?   ......_10_......

1   How many pets has she got?   ....
2   What is her dog's name?   ....
3   How many mice does she have?   ....
4   What is the name of her favourite pet?   Mr ....
5   How old is the crocodile?   ....

B Complete the man's questions.

1   How many .... have you got?

2   How many .... do you have?

3   How many .... have you got?

4   How many .... do you have?

1

3

5

18

C Let's talk about your pets!

How many .... have you got / do you have?

How many pets have you got?

Which pets would you like to have?

D Write the words in the *one* or *two* bag.

dress beaches
toys story cross
mats babies
body buses family
day tails sausage
bee classmates
meatball teddies

E Look and read. Write yes or no.

Examples

You can see a goat on the man's T-shirt. ....yes........

The door of the house is closed. ....no............

1   A frog is sitting on the dog's head. ....

2   There are two giraffes in the window. ....

3   One cat is sleeping in the tree. ....

4   You can see a crocodile in the water. ....

5   A bird is under the cow. ....

27 Food I really like!

A Bill's big breakfast.

sweets
egg food
juice
bread
peas
fruit
beans breakfast

B Write six things that Lucy likes for lunch.
Lucy likes food which has the letter 'c' in it.

....
....
....
....
....
....

C Dan's funny dinner. Look at the letters. Write the words.

1 e g g s

2 _ _ _ _ _

3 _ _ _ _ _ _

4 _ _ _ _ _

5 _ _ _ _ _ _ _

6 _ _ _ _ _ _ _ _ _

▶ **Listen and tick (✔) the box.**

What can Kim have for lunch?

1   What is May's favourite meat?

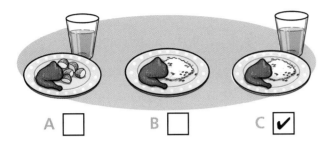

A ☐   B ☐   C ✔

A ☐   B ☐   C ☐

2   What does Alex want for breakfast today?

3   What can Hugo have for dinner?

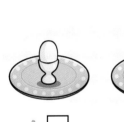 

A ☐   B ☐   C ☐

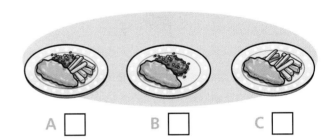

A ☐   B ☐   C ☐

4   Which drink does Anna like?

5   Which is Sue's favourite?

A ☐   B ☐   C ☐

A ☐   B ☐   C ☐

E **Listen and write the food and drink.**

I like ... ☺	I don't like ... ☹	I don't know ... 😐

F **Funtime** **Play lots of games with food!**

28 My favourite food day

A Write your answers.

Me

My favourite food is ① ....

I don't like ② .... or ....

For breakfast I eat ③ .... and ....

For lunch I drink ④ ....

For dinner I eat ⑤ ....

My favourite ice cream is ⑥ .... ice cream.

B Read the questions. Put the correct answer numbers in the yellow circles.

What's your favourite ice cream? (6)

What do you eat for breakfast? ( )

What do you drink for lunch? ( )

What's your favourite food? ( )

What food don't you like? ( )

What do you eat for dinner? ( )

C Write your friend's answers.

Name: ....

....

....

....

....

....

....

D Write your menu.

My favourite food day

breakfast	lunch	dinner
....	....	....
....	....	....
....	....	....
....	....	....

E Spell and say *onions* and *sausages*!

 on i on s

onions

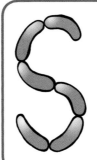 sa u sa ges

sausages

Anna puts one onion under
Sue's seven sausages!

F Read this. Choose a word from the box. Write the correct word next to numbers 1–5.

An apple

An apple is a ......*fruit*...... but it's not like an (1) .... or a banana. You can find apples in trees in some (2) .... In winter many (3) .... like eating apples! People love eating apples too, and drinking their (4) .... The (5) .... of apples are red, green or yellow. Does your family enjoy eating apple pie?

Example

fruit

colours

breakfast

juice

orange

birds

gardens

face

G *Funtime* Play the game! Food, names and animals.

29 We're in the toy shop today

A Look at the pictures and read the questions. Write one-word answers.

Examples

How many toys are in the big cupboard? ....12..........

What is the man cleaning? the .....floor.....

1 Which toy is the woman holding? a ....

2 How many people are in the shop now? ....

3 What are two of the children sitting on? a ....

4 Where are the toys now? on the ....

5 What is the man in the shop doing? ....

B Ask and answer questions about the toys.

C Look at the third story picture and read. Write yes or no.

Examples

The women are waving. ....yes......... Three people are in the shop. ....no..........

1   The horse is on the car.   ....
2   The man is sitting on a chair.   ....
3   You can see a poster on the wall.   ....
4   There are lots of bags on the floor of the shop. ....
5   The white cat is sleeping in the street.   ....

D Write the words in the boxes.

a	r	e	d	h	e	l	i	c	o	p	t	e	r

1   What's in the hat?   a ....boat.........
2   Which toys are red, white and blue?   the ....and the ....
3   What colours are on the doll's dress?   ....and ....
4   How many toys are there on the floor?   ....
5   What is standing?   the ....

E Funtime Play the game! Stand up and do it, please.

63

30 Monsters in the park

A Look at the picture. Write sentences about the monsters.

	1	2	3	4	5
A	A	water	in front of	the	behind
B	on	monster	An	tree	under
C	is	green	next to	red	flowers
D	blue	yellow	in	orange	chair

	A1	C2	B2	C1	A5	A4	B4
1	A	green	monster	is	behind	the	tree.
	A1	D1	B2	C1	A3	A4	C5
2							
	A1	C4	B2	C1	C3	A4	B4
3							
	B3	D4	B2	C1	D3	A4	A2
4							
	A1	D2	B2	C1	B1	A4	D5
5							

64

B **Listen and write the monsters' names.**

1   Mr ....
2   Mr ....
3   Miss ....
4   Mrs ....

And the red monster's name? You choose!   Miss/Mrs ....

C **In the monster hall.**

D **Where is it? Choose the right word.**

The phone is **on/in** Anna's hand.
The table is **under/on** the mirror.
The monster is **between/behind** Anna.
The chair is **in/between** the table and
the blue door.

The big lamp is **under/next to** the white door.
The mat is **in front of/on** the monster.
The books are **behind/next to** the small lamp.

E Funtime **Do the classroom quiz!**

31 Coming and going

A Look at the picture. Look at the letters. Write the words.

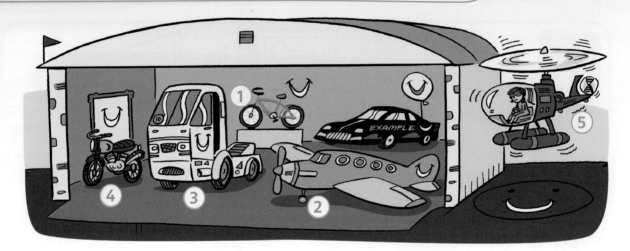

Example

c a r

1

b e i k

_ _ _ _

2

n p e l a

_ _ _ _ _

3

l o y r r

_ _ _ _ _

4

_ _ _ _ _ _ _

5

_ _ _ _ _ _ _ _ _ _

B What does Sue Smile drive, fly or ride?

Sue Smile drives her	
She flies her	
And she loves riding her	

C How do you come and go? How would you like to come and go?

I go to .... by ....

I walk to ....

I'd like to drive / ride / fly a bus / car / helicopter / lorry / motorbike / plane / train.

D Look at the picture in A. Listen and colour the smiles.

66

E Read this. Choose a word from the box. Write the correct word next to numbers 1–5.

A school bus

A school bus is big and long. A .... *man* .... or a woman drives it. In the morning you see lots of school buses in the (1)...................... with cars, bikes and (2)...................... . The bus stops next to the children's (3)...................... or flats. The children sit in the bus and put their (4)...................... on the floor. The bus goes to the school and then its (5)...................... opens and the children run to their classrooms!

Example

man

door

cow

street

houses

bags

lorries

hand

F Let's talk about the picture.

G What do you have?

I have	a great book	to	eat.
	a funny game		play.
	a new helicopter		read.
	a clean bike		drive.
	a beautiful car		ride.
	some nice sweets		fly.

32 Happy birthday!

A ▶ Listen and colour.

B Listen and draw lines.

C Answer the questions.

1 What's this?
  It's a ......cake......
2 Do you like cake?
  ....
3 What do you eat for lunch? ....
  ....

1 What's this?
  It's a ....
2 Have you got a jacket?
  ....
3 What clothes are you wearing? ....
  ....

1 What's this?
  It's a ....
2 Can you ride a horse?
  ....
3 What's your favourite animal? ....
  ....

D **Look at the picture in A. Read and write the words.**

1 You can see food and drink on this.

2 The people are in the ....

3 This is behind the people and it's big.

4 A boy's wearing a T-shirt and blue ....

5 This is closed. It's part of the house.

6 One boy has a balloon in his ....

7 There are two of them. They are standing.

8 The woman and one girl are holding these in their hands.

9 The birthday girl is wearing this on her head.

10 These are on the people's feet.

E **Look at the pictures and write the words.**

Example

s k i r t

1

_ _ _ _ _ _

2

_ _ _
_ _ _ _ _

3

_ _ _ _ _ _ _

4

5

_ _ _ _ _ _ _ _   _ _ _ _ _ _ _ _ _

What can you wear?

What can you eat?

What sport can you play?

F **Your teacher will give you a photocopy. Read about Sam and Jill.**
Write the words from E.

33 On the beach

A Draw lines.

sand

sea

beach

ball

boat

sun

fish

bird

mat

water

shell

phone

monkey

ship

B Answer questions about the picture.

C Look at the letters. Write the words. Find these things in the picture.

Example

c o c o n u t

1

t a h
  c w

_ _ _ _ _

2

o f o
 t

_ _ _ _

3

a n a n
  s b a

_ _ _ _ _ _

4

5

D What are the missing words?

What's this?   a ⁽¹⁾ ....

What colour is it?   ⁽²⁾ ....

How many ⁽³⁾ .... are there?   ....2............

What's the ⁽⁴⁾ .... doing?   ⁽⁵⁾ ....

What's this?   a ⁽⁶⁾ ....

What colour is it?   ⁽⁷⁾ ....

How many ⁽⁸⁾ .... are there?   ....4............

What's the ⁽⁹⁾ .... doing?   ⁽¹⁰⁾ ....

walking shell bird boat dog
green boats shells sleeping white

E ▶ Listen and draw lines.

Matt   Dan   May   Alice

Mark   Jill   Hugo

F Funtime Play the game! What's in your beach bag?

71

34 Let's go to the park

A Look at the picture and choose answers.

1	What is the big boy doing?	........e........	a	kicking a ball
2	Who is running?	....	b	the man
3	Who is waving?	....	c	picking up a pear
4	What is the girl doing?	....	d	the woman
5	What is the small boy doing?	....	e	flying a kite

B Read the questions. Write one-word answers.

1 Who is kicking a ball? the small ....
2 What is the man doing? ....
3 Who is picking up a pear? the ....
4 What is the woman doing? ....
5 What is the big boy flying? a ....

C ▶ Listen and colour the picture with your crayons.

D **You're in the park! Read the questions and write answers.**

1 How many people are in the park? ......
2 How many trees can you see? ......
3 Is it morning, afternoon or evening? ....
4 Who are you with? ....
5 What are you doing? ....
6 Which animals can you see? ....
7 What are you wearing? ....

E  **Read it! Write! Say it!**

Hi! Our park is great!
I can run, ... and play
with my ....
Hooray!
Let's go to the park!
Let's go today!

F *Funtime* **Play the game! Animal sentences.**

 ....

Team A | Team B

73

35 What, who and where?

A Complete the questions with Who, What or Where.
Write the answers to the questions.

1 .... 's this?   ....Tony..................
2 .... 's this?   a ....
3 ......Where...... 's the camera?   in Tony's ....

1 Who's this?   ....
2 What's she got in her hand?   a ....
3 Where's the shell?   on her ....

B Question word spelling.

Wh  's this? T  ny.

What's that?  It's a hat.

Where's your crocodile? Here or there?

C Write Where or Who in the questions.

①

1 .... is angry?
2 .... are the girls?
3 .... are the clothes?
4 .... is playing with a doll?

the mother
in Sue's bedroom
on the floor
the girls

74

D Write one-word answers.

(2)

| 5 | Where are the clothes now? | under the .... |
| 6 | Where are the books now? | in the .... |

(3)

| 7 | Who is sitting on the bed? | the .... |
| 8 | Who is opening the cupboard? | the .... |

E Questions about you.

What do you watch on TV? ....

Who watches TV with you? ....

Where is the television in your house? ....

What do you have for dinner? ....

Who has dinner with you? ....

Where do you have dinner? ....

What games do you play? ....

Who do you play with at school? ....

Where do you play in your school? ....

F ▶ Read, then listen and draw.

Monsters, monsters,

I love monsters!

My monster lamp, my monster rug, the monster on my bed.

The monsters in my toy box and in the painting on my wall.

Silly monsters, scary monsters, I love them all!

36 Great games, great hobbies!

A  **What are the missing words? You choose! Then listen to the answers.**

Kim likes playing it in the ....evening........ . She sits on her (1) .... and plays it on her new (2) .... There's an old (3) .... in it. He's catching lots of small (4) .... They're swimming in the sea. Can you see the (5) .... on their tails? Can you see the (6) .... on the tree, too? It likes eating bananas!

Kim and her (7) .... are really good at playing it. They can listen to funny (8) .... on it, too. Do you like playing computer games?

B **Look at the letters and write the words.**

 Example
r o b o t

 1 _ _ _ _ _

 2 _ _ _ _

 3 _ _ _ _

 4 _ _ _ _ _

 5 _ _ _ _ _

D **Which is Tom? Alex? Lucy? Read and draw lines.**

1

There's my friend, Tom! He enjoys fishing.

The boy with the red hair?

No! Tom's hair is black!

2

Alex is in this playground. She loves watching TV.

The girl in the really cool blue dress?

No, Alex is wearing a yellow T-shirt.

3

Lucy is here, too. She likes swimming.

The girl with the fantastic kite?

No, Lucy's got a crocodile!

E *Funtime* **Play the game! We're making long words.**

77

37 Let's play

A Look and read. Put a tick (✔) or a cross (✗) in the box.

Examples

This is a board game. ☑

These are bats. ☒

1 This is a television. ☐

2 This is a goat. ☐

3 These are jackets. ☐

4 These are bikes. ☐

5 This is a football. ☐

B What can you do with a ball? Write a, e, i, o or u.

b__ __nc__ it!   c__tch it!   h__t it!   k__ck it!   thr__w it!

C Write letters, sports and names!

a   b   c   d   e

....

a	1	Alex is at the (beach) with his grandfather today. He loves ....swimming.... !
☐	2	Anna goes to the (park.) She plays .... there.
☐	3	Sue enjoys watching .... on (television) with her family.
☐	4	Jill likes playing .... in the (playground) with her friends.
☐	5	Mark wants to play .... in the (garden) with his cousin Bill.

Which is Ben's favourite sport?

A ✔   B ☐   C ☐

1   **Which sport is Kim doing today?**

A ☐   B ☐   C ☐

2   **What is Lucy doing?**

A ☐   B ☐   C ☐

3   **What is Tom watching on TV?**

A ☐   B ☐   C ☐

4   **Where is Dan?**

A ☐   B ☐   C ☐

5   **Which girl is Sam?**

A ☐   B ☐   C ☐

E Cool! OK! Great!, Yes, please! **or** No, thanks!

Let's play
....

Jill

Do you want
to play .... ?

Mark

Would you like
to play .... ?

Sue

F Funtime **Play the game. Let's move!**

79

38 My favourites

A What are these?

boots, socks, trousers ....clothes............

1. drawing, fishing, painting ....
2. blue, green, grey ....
3. donkey, chicken, tiger ....
4. badminton, baseball, soccer ....
5. meatballs, rice, grapes ....
6. robot, doll, teddy bear ....
7. milk, fruit juice, water ....

B Ask and answer questions.

	My favourite 😊	..................'s favourite 😊	..................'s favourite 😊
animal	....	....	....
colour	....	....	....
drink	....	....	....
	....	....	....
	....	....	....
	....	....	....
hobby	....	....	....

.... are fantastic, ... is great and .... is cool!

C **Look at the pictures. Complete the sentences about Lucy.**

Lucy is nine. Her favourite colour is ......*purple*...... and her favourite toy is her .... She likes eating .... and drinking .... Her favourite animal is a .... She enjoys playing ....

D **Tell us about your friend. And your alien friend!**

.... is ....
His/Her favourite colour is .... and his/her favourite toy is his/her ....
He/She likes eating .... and drinking ....
His/Her favourite animal is a ....
He/She enjoys playing ....

E **Find and circle the American English words in the box. Then, write Pat's letter.**

s	o	c	c	e	r	f	l	f
p	t	r	e	g	r	a	y	r
c	o	l	o	r	k	v	t	i
a	s	f	c	s	t	o	r	e
n	l	r	b	s	e	r	u	s
d	v	x	m	z	b	i	c	u
y	a	i	w	q	y	t	k	f
a	p	a	r	t	m	e	n	t

Hello! My name's Tom!
I live in a **flat** next to a **sweet shop** in London. My dad drives a big **grey lorry**. My **favourite** sport is **football**. I love the **colour** blue and I love eating **chips**! Tell me about you!

Hi! I'm Pat.
I live in an .... next to a .... in New York. My dad drives a big .... My .... sport is .... I love the .... blue and I love eating .... !

F **Funtime Play the game! Let's make crosswords.**

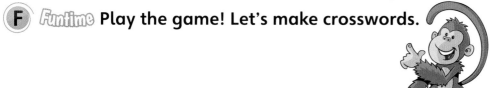

39 One foot, two feet

A Look and read. Put a tick (✔) or a cross (✗) in the box.

Examples
This is a house. ✔

 These are men. ✗

 1 This is a child. ☐

 2 These are balloons. ☐

 3 These are feet. ☐

 4 This is a mouse. ☐

 5 This is a person. ☐

B Complete the words.

C Write yes or no.

a m o u s e	lots of mice	There is one fish.	no
one foot	two f__ _t	1 There is one mouse.	....
a m__n	nine men	2 There is one woman.	....
one woman	ten wom__n	3 There is one foot.	....
a ch__ld	four children	4 There are two men.	....
one fish	lots of f__sh	5 There are two sheep.	....
a sh__ __p	seven sheep	6 There are two children.	....
one person	six p__ __ple	7 There is one person.	....

E Make sentences about the picture in D.

One	fish	are	eating	blue T-shirts.
Two	sheep	is	swimming	some bread.
Three	mice	are	running	a flower.
Four	people	are	eating	in the water.
Five	children	are	wearing	behind the dog.

F Look at the family and answer questions.

G Funtime Play the game! What's my word?

a	b	c	d	e	f	g	h	i	j	k	l	m
1	2	3	4	5	6	7	8	9	10	11	12	13
n	o	p	q	r	s	t	u	v	w	x	y	z
14	15	16	17	18	19	20	21	22	23	24	25	26

40 Night and day

A Write morning, afternoon, evening or night.

1    2    3    4

......morning......   ....

B Find words.

b	n	b	h	a	v	e	l	u	n	c	h	b	g
g	g	o	t	o	s	c	h	o	o	l	b	n	o
e	h	a	v	e	l	e	s	s	o	n	s	d	t
t	d	h	a	v	e	a	b	a	t	h	b	b	o
u	h	a	v	e	d	i	n	n	e	r	d	n	b
p	b	b	g	o	t	o	s	l	e	e	p	b	e
h	a	v	e	b	r	e	a	k	f	a	s	t	d

C Write in the or at. Write words from B under parts of the day.

.... morning	.... afternoon	.... evening	.... night
	have lunch		

D  Listen and write a name or a number.

Examples What is the boy's name?   ....Hugo....   How old is he?   ....8....

1   How many things are in Hugo's school bag?   ....
2   What is the name of Hugo's street?   .... Street.
3   What is the number of Hugo's bus?   ....
4   What is Hugo's friend's name?   ....
5   What is Hugo's teacher's name?   Mr ....

E Mark's morning. Listen and write numbers and words.

Mark's in his bedroom.

a .... ☐3️⃣

b .... ☐2️⃣

c .... ☐1️⃣

He goes to the bathroom.

d .... ☐

e .... ☐

f .... ☐

He finds his school clothes.

g .... ☐

h .... ☐

i .... ☐

He goes to the living room.

j .... ☐

k .... ☐

l .... ☐

He goes to the kitchen and has his breakfast.

m .... ☐

n .... ☐

o .... ☐

He goes to the hall and finds his school bag.

p .... ☐

q .... ☐

r .... ☐

Mark says 'Goodbye' to his ....

s

He opens the door, runs to the ....,

t

sits next to his friend, Ben, and goes to ....

u

F *Funtime* Play the game! Change places.

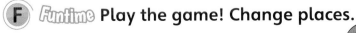

85

41 Trains, boats and planes

A Look at the picture. Make 10 words with these letters.

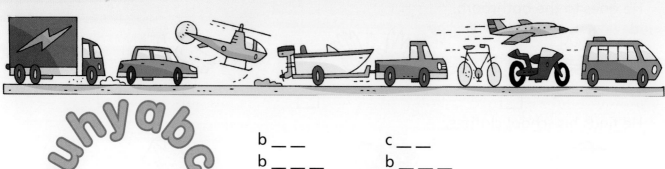

b _ _   c _ _
b _ _ _   b _ _ _
p _ _ _ _   t _ _ _ _
t _ _ _ _   l _ _ _ _
s _ _ _
m _ _ _ _ _ _ _ _ _
h _ _ _ _ _ _ _ _ _

B Look at the pictures, read the questions and write answers.

Examples

How many children are there?   ....2.........

What are the children riding?   their ....bikes.......

1 How many birds can you see?   ....

2 Where are the children now?   at the ....

3 What is the woman driving?   a ....

4 What is the boy painting?   a ....

5 What is the girl doing?   ....

C ▶ **Listen and tick (✔) the box.**

What is Pat wearing today?

A ☐   B ☐   C ✔

1   Which boy is Bill?

A ☐   B ☐   C ☐

2   Which sport is Sam playing?

A ☐   B ☐   C ☐

3   What is Tom doing?

A ☐   B ☐   C ☐

4   Where is Mum?

A ☐   B ☐   C ☐

5   How does Alex come to school?

A ☐   B ☐   C ☐

D **Talk about the picture. What can you see?**

E **Where do you want to go? Write on your ticket!**

.... ticket
from ....
to ....

PROJECT

42 About a phone

A What can you see? Write the words.

......friends...... ....

....

B Read this. Choose and write the correct word from A next to numbers 1–5.

People talk to their ......friends...... and family with it. You can take photos with it and play games with it too. It's very small and it has letters and (1) .... on it. You can find it in a store in a (2) .... in front of Mrs Bean's house. Some people put it on a (3) ...., but Mrs Bean puts it in her brown (4) .... Mrs Bean is a teacher at Lucy's (5) ....

C Say it!

I'm taking photos of me and my friend with my phone!

E ▶ Listen and colour the phones.

F Let's count! Look at the picture and write the words.

1 There are six .... *windows* .... in the houses.
2 I can see three .... in this picture.
3 There are five .... in the street.
4 I can see four .... in Mrs Bean's garden.
5 There are two .... in the fruit shop window.
6 I can see seven .... in this picture.
7 There is one .... in the car.

G *Funtime* Play the game! Listen, spell and answer.

43 What are they saying?

A Which picture? Read the sentences. Write the number of the picture.

1

Goodbye.

2

These are yours.

Thank you.

$7 \times 3 =$
$7 \times 4 =$

3

Bye!

4

This is yours.

Hooray! Thanks!

1	This is a boat.	Picture ....3....	3	This is a robot.	Picture ....
2	This is a dog.	Picture	4	This is a teacher.	Picture ....

B In which picture are they saying ...

goodbye? Picture .... and ....
thank you? Picture .... and ....

This dog is mine.

C Write his, hers or theirs.

1   The flowers are ....
2   The dog is ....
3   The boat is ....

D Draw lines between the two sentences about a person in the picture in E.

1   This young man is holding a present.
2   This woman is giving a burger to a small boy.
3   This man is waving goodbye to his grandmother.
4   This man has got a red bag. It's open and some clothes and two bottles are on the ground.
5   This old man is listening to a young boy.
6   This person is holding a man's arm.
7   This woman has got two bags.

a   He's standing next to the train.
b   She's wearing a skirt and boots.
c   He's standing in front of the burger store.
d   She's got long brown hair and she's wearing pink trousers.
e   She's wearing a pink T-shirt.
f   He's wearing a grey jacket and brown shoes.
g   He's wearing glasses.

Look at the picture. Draw lines.

F Listen and make the conversations.

G *Funtime* Play the game! What's on my card?

44 About us

A Make questions for the girl to answer.

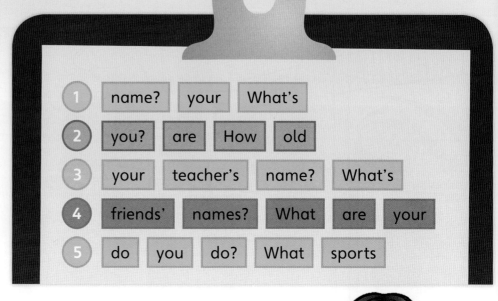

1. name? | your | What's
2. you? | are | How | old
3. your | teacher's | name? | What's
4. friends' | names? | What | are | your
5. do | you | do? | What | sports

▶ Listen and write the girl's answers.

1. ....

2. ....

3. Miss ....

4. Anna and ....

5. swimming and ....

B Which is the right answer? Draw lines.

Show me your beautiful picture.   Dad's cleaning them.

Look! We've got a fantastic new car!   Or some chocolate ones?

Can I play games on my tablet in bed?   Right! Here! Catch it!

Give me your dirty shoes!   How do you spell your name?

Sing me a sad song, please!   Which book is it in?

Ask me a question.   I only know happy ones!

Throw me that red ball, please!   Hooray! What colour is it?

Make me some lemon cakes!   He loves drawing aliens.

Read me that funny story again!   It's a fantastic jellyfish. Look!

Tell me about your brother.   No, sorry. Go to sleep now.

C Listen and tick (✔) the box.

1 Kim lives in a ... .

A ☐   B ☐

2 She goes to ... School.

A ☐   B ☐   C ☐

3 Kim is in class number ... .

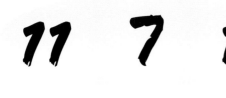

A ☐   B ☐   C ☐

4 Kim's eyes are ... .

A ☐   B ☐   C ☐

5 Her hair is ... .

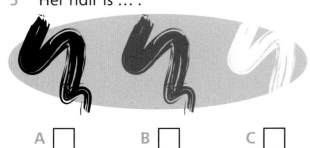

A ☐   B ☐   C ☐

6 Kim plays the ... .

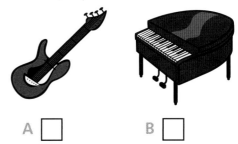

A ☐   B ☐

7 Kim's books are in the ... .

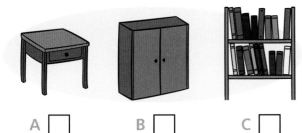

A ☐   B ☐   C ☐

8 Kim's favourite stories are about ... .

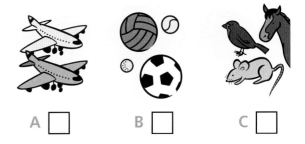

A ☐   B ☐   C ☐

D Write and talk about Nick.

E Write about you.

F Funtime Play bingo! About us!

93

45 Happy ending!

A Look at the pictures. Write the words.

B Make word groups.

wall ~~clean~~ they kite sea two | ~~green~~ night bee you hall say

bean	day	right	three	zoo	ball
clean					
green					

1

2

3

C Play the circles game!

11 Whose is it?

Learner A

Write the words for the pictures. Put a tick (✔) beside the things you have and a cross (✗) beside the things you don't have.

picture	words	Me	....
	....		
	....		
	....		
	....		
	....		
	....		
	....		
	....		
	....		

15 One, two, three animals

Write all the animals on the zoo sign.

24 What's the class doing?

Learner A

11 Whose is it?

Learner B

Write the words for the pictures. Put a tick (✔) beside the things you have and a cross (✗) beside the things you don't have.

picture	words	Me	....
	....		
	....		
	....		
	....		
	....		
	....		
	....		
	....		
	....		
	....		

24 What's the class doing?

Learner B

25 Animal challenge

What can you see in the animal picture on page 54?
Put a tick (✔) or a cross (✗) in the box.

Can you see the crocodile's tail? ✔   the giraffe's face? ✗

1	the spider's body?	☐	6	the giraffe's feet?	☐
2	the tiger's nose?	☐	7	the fish's tail?	☐
3	the hippo's legs?	☐	8	the bird's eyes?	☐
4	the monkey's arms?	☐	9	the crocodile's mouth?	☐
5	the elephant's head?	☐	10	the giraffe's ears?	☐

35 What, who and where?

41 Trains, boats and planes

What's this?

What's this?

Unit wordlist

1

animals
cat ....
dog ....
duck ....
fish ....
frog ....
goat ....
sheep ....
snake ....
spider ....

school
alphabet ....
letter ....

verbs
draw ....
say ....
spell ....

questions
What's this? ....

2

numbers
one ....
two ....
three ....
four ....
five ....
six ....
seven ....
eight ....
nine ....
ten ....
eleven ....
twelve ....
thirteen ....
fourteen ....
fifteen ....
sixteen ....

seventeen ....
eighteen ....
nineteen ....
twenty ....

possessions
ball ....
book ....
football ....
toy ....

clothes
shoe ....
sock ....

verbs
colour ....
write ....

3

names
family name ....
Miss ....
Mr ....
Mrs ....
name ....

the home
address ....
street ....

time
birthday ....

possessive adjectives
her ....
his ....
its ....

questions
How do you
spell that? ....

4

colours
black ....
blue ....
brown ....
green ....
gray/grey ....
orange ....
pink ....
purple ....
red ....
white ....
yellow ....

animals
bird ....

the home
tree ....

possessions
bike ....
boat ....
kite ....

verbs
paint ....

questions
What colour
is your hair? ....
What colour
are your eyes? ....

5

school
box ....
cross ....
example ....
line ....
no ....
question ....
sentence ....
test ....
tick ....
word ....
yes ....

animals
bee ....
polar bear ....

verbs
answer ....
put ....
tick ....

6

body and face
arm ....
body ....
ear ....
eye ....
face ....
foot ....
hair ....
hand ....
head ....
leg ....
mouth ....
nose ....
tail ....

animals
crocodile ....
elephant ....
giraffe ....
horse ....
mouse ....
zoo ....

adjectives
big ....
long ....
small ....

7

possessions
computer ....
keyboard ....
robot ....

animals
monkey ....

verbs

listen ....

look ....

run ....

see ....

sit ....

smile ....

throw the dice ....

wave ....

8

clothes

bag ....

boot ....

cap ....

dress ....

glasses ....

handbag ....

hat ....

jacket ....

jeans ....

shirt ....

shorts ....

skirt ....

trousers ....

T-shirt ....

home

chair ....

lamp ....

verbs

wear ....

adjectives

favourite ....

new ....

9

the home

flower ....

wall ....

school

story ....

verbs

drink ....

have got ....

hold ....

learn about ....

like ....

love ....

read ....

adjectives

beautiful ....

funny ....

happy ....

sad ....

scary ....

silly ....

ugly ....

adverbs

really ....

very ....

10

animals

donkey ....

pet ....

family

brother ....

cousin ....

dad ....

father ....

grandfather ....

grandma ....

grandmother ....

grandpa ....

grandparent ....

mother ....

mum ....

parent ....

sister ....

the home

flat ....

garden ....

house ....

other nouns

circle ....

verbs
live ....

prepositions
with ....

possessive adjectives
our ....
their ....

pronouns
this ....
these ....

11
possessions
balloon ....
beach ball ....
camera ....
clock ....
(computer) mouse ....
crayon ....
doll ....
drawing ....
guitar ....
paint ....
phone ....
picture ....
radio ....
teddy bear ....
tennis ball ....
thing ....
watch ....

sports and leisure
board game ....
drawing ....
music ....
skateboard ....
tablet ....

verbs
fish ....

possessive pronouns
hers ....
his ....

questions
Whose is this? ....

expressions
Pardon? ....
Sorry? ....

12
people
baby ....
best friend ....
boy ....
children ....
girl ....
kid ....
man ....
men ....
people ....
person ....
woman ....
women ....

conjunctions
or ....

expressions
Good! ....
Great! ....
Oh! ....
OK! ....
Wow! ....

13
people
classmate ....
monster ....

sports and leisure
painting ....
tennis racket ....

verbs
can ....
catch fish ....
draw pictures ....
fly ....
have a swimming lesson ....
jump ....

play badminton ....
play tennis ....
play the guitar ....
ride a bike ....
ride a horse ....
run ....
sing ....
spell really long words ....
swim ....
take photos ....
write songs ....

adjectives
good at ....

conjunctions
and ....
but ....

14
adjectives
clean ....
dirty ....
happy ....
long ....
new ....
old ....
sad ....
short ....
young ....

verbs
smile ....

questions
What's this? ....
What are these? ....

15
animals
chicken ....
cow ....
hippo ....
tiger ....

sports and leisure
ball game ....
game ....

verbs
walk ....

prepositions
in ....
next to ....
on ....
under ....

16
food and drink
apple ....
banana ....
bean ....
carrot ....
coconut ....
egg ....
fruit ....
grape ....
kiwi ....
lemon ....
lemonade ....
lime ....
mango ....
milk ....
onion ....
orange ....
pea ....
pear ....
pineapple ....
pizza ....
potato ....
tomato ....
vegetable ....
watermelon ....

verbs
eat ....

adjectives
round ....

17
food and drink
bread ....
burger ....
café ....

chicken ....

chips ....

chocolate cake ....

egg ....

fish ....

fries ....

hot chocolate ....

ice cream ....

juice ....

meatballs ....

pie ....

rice ....

sausage ....

water ....

verbs

add ....

make a drink ....

try ....

adverbs

today ....

questions

What would
you like? ....

18

the home

bathroom ....

bedroom ....

bookcase ....

desk ....

dining room ....

hall ....

home ....

kitchen ....

living room ....

mat ....

mirror ....

room ....

table leg ....

television ....

prepositions

like ....

questions

Where's your home? ....

19

the home

armchair ....

bed ....

board ....

cup ....

cupboard ....

floor ....

phone ....

piano ....

rug ....

wall ....

window ....

verbs

complete ....

20

the home

poster ....

sofa ....

places

bookshop ....

park ....

shop ....

adjectives

closed ....

open ....

tall ....

prepositions

behind ....

in front of ....

determiners

lots of ....

many ....

no ....

21

transport

bike ....

boat ....

bus ....

car ....
helicopter ....
lorry ....
motorbike ....
plane ....
ship ....
train ....
truck ....

verbs
move ....
start ....
stop ....

adverbs
again ....
here ....
there ....

22
school
classroom ....
eraser ....
page ....
paper ....
pen ....
pencil ....
playground ....
rubber ....
ruler ....
schoolbag ....
tablet ....
teacher ....

verbs
draw lines ....
take to school ....
wear glasses ....

pronouns
that ....
those ....

23
school
blackboard ....
class ....
English book ....

glasses case ....
painting ....
pencil case ....
student ....
whiteboard ....

verbs
learn English ....
sit next to ....

possessive adjectives
her ....
his ....
my ....
our ....
their ....
your ....

questions
Whose is this? ....

24
transport
rocket ....

verbs
clap ....
count ....
do a crossword ....
fish ....
go to bed ....
have a bath ....
listen to the teacher ....
make a plane ....
phone ....
point ....
sit down ....
throw a ball ....
write music ....

adjectives
double ....

expressions
Hooray! ....

25
food and drink
meat ....

107

animals
bear ....
bee ....
fly ....
insect ....
jellyfish ....
zebra ....

the world around us
grass ....
plant ....

adjectives
fat ....
wild ....

verbs
get milk ....

26
animals
pet mice ....

places
television studios ....

verbs
ask ....
talk ....

questions
How many ....
How old ....
Which pets would
you like to have? ....

27
food and drink
breakfast ....
dinner ....
lunch ....
supper ....
sweets ....

verbs
have for breakfast ....
I don't know. ....
want ....

28
food and drink
menu ....

time
day ....

verbs
drink for lunch ....
eat for breakfast ....
say ....

29
places
toy shop ....

verbs
clean ....
do ....
hold ....
sit ....
sleep ....
stand ....

adjectives
tired ....

adverbs
now ....

prepositions
between ....

30
the home
bathroom door ....
hall table ....

verbs
choose ....
pick up ....
watch TV ....

prepositions
on the wall ....
with four legs ....

31
transport
school bus ....

verbs

close ....

come to school ....

drive a car ....

fly a plane ....

go home ....

open ....

ride a motorbike ....

adjectives

nice ....

prepositions

by (bike/car) ....

questions

How do you ....
come to school? ....

32

birthdays

birthday cake ....

party ....

present ....

time

year ....

verbs

give ....

expressions

Happy birthday! ....

33

the world around us

beach ....

cloud ....

sand ....

sea ....

shell ....

clothes

beach bag ....

weather

sun ....

questions

What do you take
to the beach? ....

What do you wear
to the beach? ....

34

animals

zebra ....

verbs

choose answers ....

open a sweet ....

phone a friend ....

sing a song ....

questions

How many people
are in the park? ....
What is the boy doing? ....
Who is waving? ....

expressions

Let's go to the park! ....

35

adjectives

angry ....

right ....

verbs

have dinner ....

play with dolls ....

prepositions

on TV ....

pronouns

that ....

this ....

questions

What? ....

Where? ....

Who? ....

36

sports and leisure

computer game ....

hobby ....

screen ....

body and face

teeth ....

verbs

enjoy ....

swim in the sea ....

37

sports

badminton ....

baseball ....

basketball ....

hockey ....

table tennis ....

tennis ....

verbs

bounce ....

catch ....

go fishing ....

go swimming ....

hit ....

kick ....

prepositions

at the beach ....

on television ....

expressions

Cool! ....

Great! ....

No, thanks! ....

Yes, please! ....

38

sports and leisure

baseball bat ....

drawing ....

fishing ....

hockey stick ....

painting ....

toys

alien ....

teddy bear ....

British and American words

chips – fries ....

colour – color ....

favourite – favorite ....

flat – apartment ....

football – soccer ....

grey – gray ....

lorry – truck ....

shop – store ....

sweet – candy ....

39

irregular plurals

child – children ....

fish – fish ....

foot – feet ....

man – men ....

mouse – mice ....

person – people ....

sheep – sheep ....

woman – women ....

40

time

afternoon ....

day ....

evening ....

morning ....

night ....

verbs

get up ....

go to bed ....

go to sleep ....

put on clothes ....

say goodbye ....

wash ....

prepositions

at night ....

in the morning ....

questions

When? ....

expressions

Good afternoon! ....

Good morning! ....

Hello! ....

Hi! ....

41

transport

ticket ....

wheel ....

verbs
play hockey ....

prepositions
at the beach ....
from ....
in our car ....
on the bus ....
to ....

42
places
phone shop ....
shop door ....
store ....

verbs
find ....
take photos of a friend ....
talk to a friend ....

adjectives
correct ....

prepositions
at school ....
in a store ....

expressions
Right! ....

43
food and drink
bottle ....
burger store ....

places
station ....

verbs
wave goodbye ....

expressions
Bye! ....
Don't worry! ....
Goodbye ....
Good evening ....
Here you are. ....
I don't understand. ....
Me too! ....
Oh dear! ....

See you! ....
That's right. ....
Well done! ....

personal pronouns
I .... me ....
he .... him ....
she .... her ....
it .... it .... its ....
we .... us .... ours ....
you .... you ....
they .... them ....

44
verbs
ask a question ....
make a cake ....
read a lot ....
show me a picture ....
tell us a story ....
try new food ....
write stories ....
write with your
left hand ....

prepositions
about ....

45
sports and leisure
counter ....
dice ....
end ....
start ....

body and face
part of your body ....

school
letters of the
alphabet ....

time
part of the day ....

verbs
clap ....

questions
What now? ....